HARD
EVIDENCE

TIMOTHY LIU

HARD EVIDENCE

TALISMAN HOUSE, PUBLISHERS
JERSEY CITY, NEW JERSEY

Published in the United States of America by
Talisman House, Publishers
P.O. Box 3157
Jersey City, New Jersey 07303-3157

Manufactured in the United Sates of America
Printed on acid-free paper

ISBN: 1-58498-022-2 (paper); 1-58498-023-0 (cloth)

ACKNOWLEDGMENTS:

The poems in this book first appeared in the following publications: *American Letters & Commentary, American Voice, Antioch Review, Asian Pacific American Journal, Bellingham Review, BOMB, Boston Book Review, Boulevard, Chelsea, Colorado Review, Columbia Poetry Review, Confrontation, Denver Quarterly, Fence, First Intensity, Gettysburg Review, Global City Review, Heart Quarterly, Iowa Review, Kenyon Review, Massachusetts Review, Mid-American Review, New American Writing, Paris Review, Parnassus: Poetry in Review, Pequod, Ploughshares, The Progressive, Quarterly West, Rhizome, Ribot, River Styx, Salmagundi, Seneca Review, Solo, Sulfur, Sundog, Talisman, Tin House, TriQuarterly, Verse, Volt,* and *Western Humanities Review.*

Some of these poems also appeared in the following e-zines: *Can We Have Our Ball Back* (canwehaveourballback.com), *Electronic Poetry Review* (www.poetry.org), *nowCulture* (www.nowculture.com), *Poetry Daily* (poems.com), *Shampoo* (shampoopoetry.com), and *Slope* (www.slope.org).

Heartfelt thanks to Bruce Beasley, Chris Davis, Ed Foster, Linda Gregg, and Jane Mead. As always, this book is for Christopher Arabadjis—*Spur nur dich allein.*

Library of Congress Cataloguing-in-Publication Data
can be found at the end of this book.

CONTENTS

I.

Ars Poetica . . . 5

Nostalgia . . . 6

An Evening Train . . . 7

Survivors . . . 8

The Marriage . . . 11

The Assignation . . . 12

Coup de Grâce . . . 13

Legend . . . 14

Happy Valley . . . 15

Dog Days . . . 16

The War . . . 17

Lovesong . . . 18

Orpheus and Eurydice . . . 19

Winter . . . 20

A Large Spacious Field Where We Can Sit Zazen . . . 21

For a New Century . . . 22

II.

To Calamus . . . 27

III.

Hard Evidence . . . 49

Big Boy . . . 50

Glimpsed through Speeding Glass . . . 51

Reading Sappho . . . 52

Reading Catullus . . . 53

A Song of Experience . . . 54

Not Marble nor the Gilded Monuments . . . 55

With One Eye Open . . . 56

Pretty Please . . . 57

Remote Control . . . 58

Self-Portrait as Mall Rat . . . 59

Tabula Rasa . . . 60

Sestina . . . 61

Kiss and Tell . . . 63

A Mighty Fortress . . . 64

To Zion . . . 65

Kingdom Come . . . 67

An Inferno . . . 68

IV.

Ex Nihilo . . . 71

In Fear . . . 72

Against Nature . . . 74

Habeas Corpus . . . 75

Till Death Do Us Part . . . 76

Winter . . . 78

A Rendezvous . . . 79

Next Day . . . 80

Noli Me Tangere . . . 81

In Flagrante Delicto . . . 82

Walking Alone at Ocean's Edge . . . 90

V.

Ars Poetica . . . 93

Courtly Inscriptions Inked on Jute . . . 94

Splinters from the Tree That Lightning Struck . . . 95

After the Funeral . . . 96

Consolation . . . 97

Ghost Ranch . . . 98

Georgia O'Keefe: American Icon . . . 99

Looking West . . . 100

The Long Boat . . . 101

Emptying the Mind . . . 102

Sitting Naked on a Porch . . . 103

Knowing When To Stop . . . 104

Passing through the Enchanted Circle . . . 105

A Minor Distraction . . . 106
Easter, 1997 . . . 107
Approaching the Buddha . . . 108
Many Mansions . . . 109
Middle-Class Realia as Iconographic Vanitas . . . 110
Reading the Book of Odes Late at Night . . . 111
Western Wars Mitigated by the Analects . . . 112

Faith slips—and laughs, and rallies—
Blushes, if any see—
Plucks at a twig of Evidence—
And asks a Vane, the way—

—Emily Dickinson (#501)

HARD EVIDENCE

I.

Ars Poetica

Childhood begins with your first good line—
a spider waiting for its kill,

                            moon-blind moths
turned back into a blood cocoon. How to feed
such appetite

                trapped in its solarium of air—
eight-eyed and benign in a jar full of holes?
Let Jesus wait

                as Lazarus did in the tomb,
childhood like that row of mummies we saw
at the Rosicrucian Museum—

                            the one undone
charred to the bone, its bed of linen wraps
our future

                as each of us assumed the shape
of a hieroglyph inside the walls of that model
cobwebbed crypt

                    more real than any Bible
story we knew by heart—hands touching
those ruins

                when no one else was looking.

Nostalgia

The weight of summer fruit in a gilded frame.

Or heads cast down to jars of anthurium.

Nothing like crystal kissed by random nicks.

Forgotten rhythms of salt and blood as rawhide gives.

The glass demanding that your face be seen.

Be made an example of.

Against his hirsute wrist a song we cannot sing.

Those fists that congregate at the site.

Nor gather at Waterloo while Napoleon comes and goes.

Iron rails where a fall should have been.

Some valentines torn open after a sudden rain.

An Evening Train

whistles past hacked-down fields of corn,
heading towards a boy who whittles
an effigy of himself. We go on sleeping
through sirens and crimson strobes
that flash on remains no one can identify
till we line up at dawn to see who's
missing. At the zoo this morning, a girl
found half-devoured in a moat, two lions
licking their chops, *Little Rock, Arkansas*
the only proof left on her body to show
how far she was from home. A tattered copy
of *The Odyssey* later found in her purse.
Did she love her life? We warn our children
not to lay their heads down on the tracks
in wintertime, knowing how it's not
always best to know what's coming our way.

Survivors

Never seem to hear the alarm
(after thrusting all of his)
go off. The slightest touch
(secret rage into my body)

after thrusting all of his
(will startle my tongue awake)
secret rage into my body
(flying across the airport)

will startle my tongue awake
(our bedroom filled with cries)
flying across the airport
(terminal—we felt forced)

our bedroom filled with cries
(spent on therapy and self-help)
terminal—we felt forced
(to put on our best smiles)

spent on therapy and self-help
(books stacked beside our bed)
to put on our best smiles
(as we boarded the plane—words)

books stacked beside our bed
(that keep me up until four)
as we boarded the plane—words
(meant nothing to my skull)

that keep me up until four
(each night reeking of alcohol)
meant nothing to my skull
(crashing upside Plexiglas)

each night reeking of alcohol
(like a dream that will dissolve)
crashing upside Plexiglas
(our sense of time remained)

like a dream that will dissolve
(or a childhood we never had)
our sense of time remained
(distorted—as if those faces)

or a childhood we never had
(suddenly started to crawl)
distorted—as if those faces
(passing through a Jetway)

suddenly started to crawl
(up the chimney, black sheep)
passing through a Jetway
(with all that baggage in tow)

up the chimney, black sheep
(without a shepherd. As if love)
with all that baggage in tow
(belonged to a silent movie)

without a shepherd. As if love
(never seem to hear the alarm)
belonged to a silent movie
(go off. The slightest touch)

shot years ago could go on—

The Marriage

A redwing blackbird exploding in the mirror
of a semi hauling cattle down I-80. Darling,
what we would give for a troop of boy scouts
traipsing through the woods. The self as idol

waiting for worship. A cold front coming on.
Piss holes drilled into snow by feral dogs.
Our marriage stalled again, nothing but blue
sparks arcing across corroded jumper cables.

The Assignation

Overshadowed by the sound of a beak
scraping cuttlebone, smell of sperm

in that room where crushed saltines
were whistled out of open mouths—

a mermaid carved into the headboard
of an antique bed still whispering

to that married man who had not yet
made up his mind. Were we ever able

to inhabit the paradise hour replete
with kisses steeped in votive wine?

Never seem strong enough to tear up
the letters while birds flew overhead—

bodies pushed through zones of cold
as we dove down deeper into the river.

Coup de Grâce

Bodies made solid by weights succumb
to illness. Years of focussed practice

lost in that afternoon of neglect.
What we are felt after the fact—

walls with his name graffitied on them,
late night actors who could've been

his double. Dolls left in a drawer
unopened for years like those boxes

of books in the attic that became
our inheritance. The things loved least

loved at last. Weather vanes renewed
by wind. But the former tenants are gone.

Our words a bridge. Just as my kiss
once sealed the tomb of his empty mouth.

Legend

No sign that you were coming after me.
An hour glass tipped over. That spine
I cracked on a book on sex discarded

under the bed. Knives left untouched
in the cutlery block. Only that sound
of apples falling into an empty well.

Happy Valley

Workers milk the unsheathed phallus
of a horse. Body as machine. Couples

rocking on decrepit chairs, humming
hymns devoid of God as mayflies

swarm a swimming hole where a car
careened out of control—that farm

in Amherst harvesting sperm a source
of bliss. It all comes down to this.

Excess. Like that glass of lukewarm
water spat from the mouths of Elders

trying to pass us up on the right—
handlebars askew as they readjust

their clip-on ties, a radio blasting
oldies that all of us used to sing

till someone broke the antenna off.

Dog Days

Cruising potholed streets from dusk
to dawn—bottles of Absolut rolling
on a backseat floor where dreams

went up in smoke. Barbecued ribs
transporting us from freezer burn
to voracious mouths yawing wide

for tinder gathered by rosy campfire
girls—stalks of corn "knee-high
by the Fourth of July" we used to say

with all of our fuses lit—the future
halfway up the sky as bottle rockets
turned the neighbor's house to ash.

The War

Ants picking off those aphids sucking
green spirea shoots,
                    buds blistering
on stalks of towering hollyhocks
brought down by the wind—
                         veiled threats
like a boot heel crushing radishes
underfoot. A world
                where a bleach blond
fingers his bulge, ivy cascading down
that brick façade
              to schoolyard desks
that have come unhinged. No lessons
to be mastered now,
                only a field
full of Shirts and Skins, and we root
for Skins, whatever
                  summer strips down
to its barest form—limbs and torsos
on opposing teams
              tangled in the grass.

Lovesong

A crowded hillside covered with snow.

As feathers fall.
As birds wheel past an empty pulpit.
Where motes of nations lodge in the moon's cold eye.

Testify we've traveled there and back.

A totaled matchbox car.
Four good wheels grounded in a ditch.
With our tongues laid out like relics in a tomb.

Orpheus and Eurydice

You and I not sleeping—a preacher
slamming gin and tonics in the back of a church
　　　made out of glass: the TV louder
　　　　　than nine muses mouthing a garland hammered out
　　　of gold. Such evangelical zeal
as we channel-surf on a bed that comes unmoored
　　　each night—discs of breath dissolving
　　　　　on revolving doors still turning in the lobby
　　　of our hotel—a flag at half-staff
wrapping itself tighter and tighter around its
　　　frozen pole. Some said the reading was
　　　　　well-attended, the only vacant seat belonging
　　　to that woman who had plunged her heels
through a skylight while doing the rumba on top
　　　of a roof floodlit by a billboard—
　　　　　shards of glass embedded in the ankles of that
　　　Russian émigré who lay spread-eagle
on someone's kitchen floor, her lover peering down
　　　through the hole that her body made.

Winter

A bare bulb swinging
on the porch, my lashes

laced with ice. Charred
dahlias encased in brick

on a sidewalk strewn
with rinds. Words eddy

in the air, kissless
days that wander far

from the house. *If love
should lose its narrative—*

no sweetness left in
your breath's dispatch.

A Large Spacious Field Where We Can Sit Zazen

Children behind the trailer park
up to their necks in snow,
vapor trails crisscrossing across the sky
while cowbirds roost on a silo
eaten out by rust—you
and I passing through this scene at eighty
miles per hour with the radio off—
a farm house sawn in half
on the bed of a semi kicking up dust
along that two-lane road—the radio
off—a smokestack smoking
on the horizon. Nothing here to feed
our jobless mouths, only the eggs
of cowbirds crowding out
the nests of songbirds who return each spring
to Southern Illinois—you and I
now passing through this scene
while a river pushes through the windows
of a school bus stuck all season
at the bottom of some
ravine, the voices of children screaming
tell us what to do—a farm house
sawn in half—this journey
almost down to its final cigarette.

For a New Century

The authors have been winnowed.

This anthology proves it.

A century in the palm of your hand.

What to do with the other.

Disengaged the clutch the motor revs.

The road he said the road.

Potpourri scattered across the dash.

*

Now returning to the zone where a table fades
into background noise, where a conversation
scatters at the site of a falling bomb—

A kind of poetry the century was ever after
as lovers strolled through parks cruised
after dark when it was safe to come out—

(come out come out wherever you are)

The decades that it took to rebuild. And if
the song overhead in the crowns of the trees
is not the same song, only an approximation—

As wheel refused a road that swerved into
an aftermath of strobes, its calculus
but an epitaph chiseled onto stone—

(stone the centuries cannot roll away)

This too your Appalachia. This too a rebus strip
with nineteen strings and seven holes rocking up

against the birth door, a viola de gamba lodged
between the knees—what scholars have called

a new world only an approximation, a fragment of song
while bagpipes rode out West across the Crusades—

trumpets heralding apocalypse in the good book,
charred edges mapping out the earth's four corners—

four centuries of the English tongue from King James
to Hip Hop inside a labyrinth of limbs strobe-lit

into dawn where taxis lumber down Times Square—
newsprint torn loose from a sleeping form, want

ads floating upward on a draft of pigeons flying
straight into the sluice of Diamond Row—

(stone the centuries cannot roll away)

(wherever you are)

A few doors down: a child fingering worn-out
spines (WISE MEN FISH HERE) asks his father
who Ezra Pound was. "A Nazi," the voice replies—

(a fragment of song at century's end)

Harpes et luz. The decades that it took
to rebuild. And the song refused at last

like a lottery ticket trampled underfoot—
Ignatow   Levertov   Laughlin   obits

floating in cyberspace as each of us are
on a monitor screen unstrung to the nines—

*

Clearing now an aerial view.

Winnowing the hired hands below.

Quill that trues the plough.

Summon them.

Begin again at the singed spine.

Ashen up the open flue.

Ever slouching towards the site.

II.

cal a mus (kal ə məs), n. 1. the sweet flag, *Acorus calamus*. 2. its aromatic root. 3. any of various tropical Asian palms of the genus *Calamus*, which are sterile on Western soil. 4. the hollow base of a feather; a quill. [1350-1400; ME < L < Gk *kálamos* reed, stalk]

To Calamus

I. Psalm

A slow smoke through the barest twigs.

Flint and steel strewn on that tinder path.

Fear not the days the nights the leaves

dissolve. Or faint resolve. So what

if bellies of winter geese fly overhead

as we begin to forget our lines . . .

Others come to take our place. A sign

to hurl our hoard of stones against

when schools let out with their screams

and bells. Take heart. A fountain pen

runs dry in the middle of the road.

As pages of some Promethean text riffled

by the wind. By evening it is gone—

everything that we own less than the moon.

II. Denouement

Letters I have saved sealed inside

an envelope of flame—luxurious

obsequies that pander to some base

desire time exhausted: *Su, straniero,*

il gelo che dà foco, che cos'è?

No news from you, nor signatures

resembling tenderness, only bellicose

notes that rise from memory's trough—

lust betrothed to spectral gleaning

in a mind where fear left tiny scars,

the postman's bootprints puncturing

a foot-thick crust of snow as lovers

disrobe behind a shower curtain

appliquéd with giant yellow daisies.

III. New Life

Whether you get down on your knees

or not. Wild mint. Gopher holes.

But mostly grass in all directions

across the prairie should you remain

standing where you are. No use

in trying to belong to this: two posts

supporting a gilded frame—empty

whichever way you look through it.

Always just beyond. The unsleeved arms

of men working soil that had slept

all winter. Molar click at dawn

signaling the slow arrival of spring

as we toss and turn in bed—seeds

now splitting open in the dark loam.

IV. To Renew

Or else. And if the book tears or cracks

or wants to be resewn into

its binding. Yet words that lie within

get dusted off. (your breath) *Touch me*

not whispered behind a row of stiff

Brancusi pedestals so that

this want might be contained. (that lie

within) Syringa song on the tongue

of Philomel. To rue. And if you

touch me not, your breath will do—

some gravid phthisic baldachin

buried long enough, words renewed

by a voice that feeds me in this dire

hour of need. (so that this want)

V. The Poem as Incarnation of Bodily Want

Eden we never knew but Calvary.

Nailed into place as the ravens

dove down. Must one sing until

the end? How else abhor that hyssop

dipped in pitch. Or rosary beads

that roll right off the tongue if one

could only speak. Command. Touch

the robes of the Simoniac Pope

consumed in flames. Heart's travail.

Starched lapels of a schoolboy's

uniform. His majesty. "My God"

cried out on St. Gertrude's soiled

knees—copious ejaculate a sign

of Being. The whole room lit with it.

VI. Prothalamion

Notes that tremble in the chalice

of a diva's throat. Tendrils overtaking

a live oak split to the stump

as nature's downward spiral plummets

into a ditch. No affairs. Nothing

but our bodies in a bridal bed

creaking on the weathered springs.

What ripens on the sill? Sixes. Sevens.

And all those times we watched

the garden come to an end, the ground

turned over. Grapes in the arbor

rotting on the vine, the stereo on

the blink—no music in this house

but a broken queen-size bed. New wine.

VII. The Marriage

Sparks fly off a love well past its prime

a music that escapes from some cracked

wedding glass voicing long forgotten

tunes my mother's heart the rise and fall

each time I ride your chest your sex

the only soundtrack in this house lean close

enough to hear that quickened pulse

like flood like wine sloshing in its sluice

a dissonant ear those drunken tongues

floating inside that cavernous dark you call

your life get born arrest the eye reverse

the flow of light each time we turn

back into that christened world where claw

and tooth rub up against the inner wall.

VIII. Scenic Vista

A few words. The phone uncradled

in a piss-stained booth while a stranger

hammers me with his hips, nailing

my body down through the god-hole.

The hood still hot to touch—exhaust

caught in the choke hold of a burning

manifold. Pure machine. My ass

releasing its grip as lubed shocks

slow to a shudder. Stray bullets

riddling cold aluminum siding

in a shanty town twice risen

from collapse—our voices heavy

as hooves stampeding into stardust

while lights go out in the valley below.

IX. That Vinegar Hyssop Raised to His Lips

The bones picked clean intensifying

absence. Neither the blue Aegean

nor the cliffs of Corfu were enough

for the men who had slept between us.

If winter had not come. Vases

auctioned off as part of his estate.

Effluvium. All that minuscule

ephemera we called the war caught

in the water's sheen cascading down

a cutting board nicked with tiny cuts.

His wrists. A rendezvous near pay phones

as sirens doppler through the skull.

The day's aperture widens. My pulse

now swelling hard in the blood sluice.

X. Martyrs

Where crowds assemble, one must hone

a patience equal to the day's

stigmata—places in the world left

undefiled while oratory falls

on deafened ears. Oiled panels

hewn from forests hosting parades

of academic regalia, mortar boards

askew. A mock cortege. Anathema

where genitals swell under robes

that sway to the organ's thundering

tremolo. How we fan ourselves

with hymnals beneath a colloquy

of bells and broken glass—a burning

in our bosoms as the arrows fly.

XI. Prophecy

The Baptist's head rising from that din

of notes *not meant to be heard.* As if.

Hair hanging down to make a jail

of his face. Trails of cloud as chariots

race across a field where spectators

dine on canapés and petits fours

to some waltzes on an old Victrola

missing its crank. A world without God

like a gilded throne sans antimacassars?

No hairshirts needed where jacuzzis

effervesce as we cruise that suburban

sprawl—manicured lawns choked with thrips,

neighbors peeking through the shutters

for one last glimpse of anything.

XII. No Vacancy

tourists past peak the seasons last

an ashtray full or a sidewalk trashed

with dirty looks and a pile of books

falls off the dash accelerate past

empty billboards those greasy fries

wilting at the bottom of an extra

value meal why not admit it took

this world an entire age to produce

a michelangelo an aleatory sign

at eighty miles per hour with power

windows down fag hags kissing ass

at the county morgue big toes tagged

like dreams tucked in a motel bed

magic fingers running up our spines

XIII. A Song of Experience

a sword now comes to disturb the peace

as school desks bolted to the ground

shake loose where rhinestones on tiaras

fall a kind of disgrace while drag

queens preen down hometown parades

in sequined spandex shorts on asphalt

runways running through the heart

of the bible belt where billy clubs

swing between our legs as we rise

to that chorus of *is* our voices nothing

without go-go boys and belly jewels

strummed on a harlot's zither burning

roods blazing into view where viral

crusades ram steel rods into our doors

XIV. Sometimes Sex

Sometimes a look shot from a pretty jock.

Or cock or balls or tits or ass or taste

of cunt on the tip of a married prick.

Mostly trolls. Sometimes talk or a wad

of bills bulging in a redneck's denims.

To suck or to be sucked. Sometimes size.

Or a tapping foot—shorts pulled down

to the ankle bone. That smell of dis-

infectant glistening over bathroom tile.

Seldom glory. Mostly hole. Ever seated

for hours on end—ass meat burning red

on a public toilet seat. Sometimes blood.

Or bruise or death you never know what

kind of love. Even a dream. Come. True.

XV. An Inferno

Unable to find our way back home because.

The childhood road is always doomed you must.

States of mind we drive and drive unable.

Did you come to die or die to come here?

Forget California Iowa no bridge between.

The gravestones do their work. No caskets

floating underneath the surface of the earth's

skin. Nor mausoleums erected six feet

above the ground as in New Orleans doing

drag down Bourbon Street the night the Parade

Disco burned to the ground. "Disco Inferno."

Even if it was the Eighties playing tag

the fag with all those flitting catamites

caught between disco new wave techno house.

XVI. Stylus

unable to attract our work disturbed

by so much inattention: hunger

inside those hours you thrust and thrust

so little work so much attention

undisturbed (transcend) unnoticed

yes the body says what is enough

come closer but the mind you are

a diamond tip dissolving nothing less

a worn-out groove walled-in by sound

(spiral ever skating toward the center)

(spindle threaded through the god-hole)

underneath your voice: cowardice

and the grave and under that your love

relent repent relent relent relent

XVII. Exultate Jubilate

fire in that square floodlit by crimson

gels left onstage a floating red silk

scarf that snaked around the nimblest calves

unable to outlast Mozart's legacy

or Pater's gemlike flame abandoned dream

erased by edicts of the blood the song

the space with both feet off the ground

if only for a moment elephantine

memory as the curtain falls full weight

the voice of Kathleen Battle amplified

fades away five years to the day and still

your body as it was caught between

Isadora and the wheel and not what it has

become a form that those who live must bear

XVIII. Memorial

Missile pops now melting at the base

of three bronze Adonises—rifles in tow

against flak jackets stiff with art's rigor

mortis. Names etched in glass. In stone.

The dissonance of a Sol LeWitt hanging

in the Holocaust Museum. This poem

unable to compete with Yevtushenko's

"Babi Yar." Or a pile of shoes. Disney

and dioramic cattle cars breaking down

cold rhetoric—Karadzic on the slopes

with camera crews. Wherever he goes

is news—booby-trapped dolls a blow

to the Dayton Peace Accord. Suicide

bombers well on their way to heaven.

XIX. Figures on a Human Scale

So it was a disaster: butterfly nets

in the hands of children racing

through a landscape sown with buried

mines. Did someone say their bodies

looked like "flowers opening"?—

cries and shouts from a common crowd

gone mute. Regard the fallen form!

Manet's *Dead Toreador* cut out

from a larger scene. Yet would we

mar eternity with the oil from

our fingertips?—a portrait by Vermeer

shoved into a waiting van, our faces

still held captive by what remains

unsolved. All that we could not save.

XX. Vox Humana

Wrapped in scarves of flame, a woman

sealed in a pinewood box offering

prayers to a God she was not afraid

to meet. Are we nothing more

than names still searching for voices

to inhabit?—Giuditta Pasta,

Maria Malibran, and all those divas

who survive as print, fioriture

of portraiture long before our age

reduced their gowns to relics enshrined

behind smoked glass—La Fenice's pyre

devouring sheaves of Callas' letters

as we gondola downstream—ashes

blown back into our faces.

III.

Hard Evidence

A room walled-in by books where hours withdraw.

At the foot of an unmade bed a bird of paradise.

Motel carpet melted where an iron had been.

His attention anchored to a late-night glory hole.

Of janitorial carts no heaviness like theirs.

Desire seen cavorting with the yes inside the no.

A soul kiss swimming solo in an open wound.

The self as church where the whores now gather in.

Big Boy

where polka dots mask a mastiff's bullet-ridden hide
rote prayer that sinecure we temp to pass the time
in scenes unfit for viewing love freed from its script

no time to search for trump cards vanity plays in vain
where ankles dangle high above those sure calamities
now breaking in that ghetto on stiletto heels we strut

as ski lifts avalanche into the mind's unshingled calm
fear not the shots on kodak paper boys jack-off upon
ass meat spread in centerfolds a canine wrenches free

Glimpsed through Speeding Glass

zipped-up in duffel bags some newborn twins

mistaken for kittens mewling in subzero weather

miles from the nearest town inconsequential

where pistol shots ricochet off iron doors

St. John the Divine or a human hair stretched

tight inside a hygrothermograph monitoring air

that consumes a ready-made the future taken

hostage as each man tests his own chameleon

appetite in rivers made of flesh that undulate

on a marble floor our waking life but a fragment

of the dream where fishhooks catch in throats

where children plant a thousand pines more

lasting than these lines some gas jets flaming

out at the county morgue my eyes looking over

a commuter's shoulder the *Lyrica Graeca* left

on a vacant seat in that daily rush devoured

without sustenance the hours now slipping past

Reading Sappho

hurt me hear if ever hearing from afar
the house grief is to touch a boy because

ungarlanded easy rival come to me to musk
now blowing here sweet and softer roses

than this nectar tear your shirt I want
what leapt-up eagerly climbed on unmarried

stallions in praise best slender branch
reddens at the tip your face beyond all

others with hyacinth lift high the groom
again farewell you who injure me most

underfoot the ground all purple never
lyre upon my breast your laughter subtle

fire to be endured no pleasure in dew-wet
cheeks cruel gift or say what you love best

Reading Catullus

eased of gold attendant honey swallows up
all swelling eyes you stood my boat behind

the port your waters saw the oar-blades first
to lee a god where silphium might slake

unwilling hard against no more I'll watch
the last light-hearted buttonholes undone

as small talk pried uncouth that rickety
bridge over river-mud a ruse cavorting

leap-frog rocked in the crook of maidenhead
nor has he risen up as dolt-like lethargy

disputes a pederast tossed about his cottage
sheltered from overdrafts of ruinous sort

straight-faced the length received it duly
no less large the sight munificence possessed

A Song of Experience

A headless doll floating in a barnyard trough.

Time to kill where daughters circle on tilted bicycle wheels.

Three times round the mortgaged house as fire ants march on.

Nozzle of a gas can lowered to the ground.

If lust should strike a match in that dark no longer dark.

A hair shirt drying on a chair beside the hearth.

A satellite dish keeping score.

Kite as key as lightning bolt as hirsute knuckles strike.

Like dates on granite markers veiled with moss.

The touch that follows bliss or bruise some said ninety-proof.

Illegible stars scrawling their way across the sky.

Nothing left for us to read.

Childhood's charred pages floating gently up the flue.

Not Marble nor the Gilded Monuments

Gone the old world governed by oaths / honor
power-broken by Branagh and his crew
in Dolby sound / Saxo Grammaticus
giving birth to Amlet via lost Elizabethan
scripts where lads in tights sporting plumes
forsake their usual coffee-house ennui /
not mopes who genuflect but men of action
whose hedonistic juices clue us in
to moral voids catapulting tumult
into catastrophic spheres where brassy
salvos toll bravissimo as we clamber
back into a childhood retold by Livy
where countless artifacts are strewn about
a theater emptied of such bric-a-brac
handed down / a tattered cloak left
hanging on a director's chair / a rupture
with the past / helicopters on fire
outside a reconstructed Globe / no signs
of Olivier as a new Lear stumbles over
rain-torn maps magic-markered onto enormous
sheets of butcher paper those artisans
unroll / rote readings gliding over gnarled
syntax more burden than delight for masses
raised on MTV's complacent pageantry
of star-crossed lovers / Baz Luhrmann's
soundtrack now outselling the Bard himself
at a local Barnes & Noble where we pay
lip-service to classics filtered through
that cauldron of echo-chambered voices
on sets backdropped with Warhol's Jackie O.

With One Eye Open

A meltdown of pictorial signs.

Odalisque as playmate in that age of spectacle.
Marius and Jugurtha mere shadows on a screen.

Buy de Kooning.   Sell Dine.

Trafficked to new publics "to stimulate desire."
Some offshore feathers coated with crude
afloat on the nightly news.

More savvy than. Connected to. Never having read.

To end where the world begins uncritical of the real.

Twenty-six gas stations a forgotten alphabet.
The West a vast horizon staging "beauty underfoot."

"I am nature."   "I am culture."

That crisis called an easel—
ideograms on a canvas done with piss
or charlatans who seal their own shit in a can.

"What you see is what you see."

Pretty Please

tens of thousands of bathers floating on ghats
additional support for [   ] provided by

housewives hot for mongoose pie tossing garlands
made of marigolds down paths as jazz and blues

converge [   ] cultures grown in incubators
soon clap in unison against Malthusian struggles

improvise on biogas and [   ] swirling past
[   ] to the drone of sitars plucked at dawn

raw sewage turning into another round of applause
an expansion of [   ] or algae blooms

if forced to take a holy dip well then why not
with future populations scheduled to overtake

[   ] sans accoutrements such [   ]
marching to the high-pitched squeal of a fax

machine where dancers [   ] offstage
site-specific enginerring plans wrestling sacred

cows in tutus trapped inside a mahatma's cordless
phone [   ] as TV credits scroll down

Remote Control

A presidential motorcade sponsored by Nabisco.

Bloody outbreaks of Ebola now showing at.

You've got some Royal Caribbean coming.

Correspondents left incommunicado.

Revlon girls ejecting from twin-engine planes.

Effective relief without the gas.

Croatians rounded-up on busses heading towards.

Stalin's widow trampled by the masses she.

No end to all this footage exported from.

Most certainly will appeal the.

Every hour on the hour the Energizer bunny.

Self-Portrait as Mall Rat

anchored to a wall of monitors flanking
food courts unallied with any school /
amazons donning whale-bone girdles
but a fragment of the dream in a bygone
era more real than poses stiffening
inside last year's catalog / more
tokens in my pockets than winter coats
stolen off the racks when security looks
the other way / Dear Sirs / how many
hoops before you see me as I am not as
you will / old trolls still lurking
behind toilet stalls clutching twenty-
dollar bills in search of virgin ass
tucked inside a sailor suit afloat
off-center in the far corner of an eye
caught between waves of sleep receding
into an evening ever-plagued with
melancholia waltzing through rooms full
of what we dare not own / my kingdom
for a coat / for some lurid tourists
in towering heels yet able to overwhelm
the Übermensch / not boys hauled-off
in handcuffs for being at odds with
vanguard trends trying to drown out
the loneliness we all must feel inside
that sea of glass displays where droves
of replicants stand ready now to serve

Tabula Rasa

Cancel our appointments to greet
a stranger who never arrives?

Surrender now for half an hour
to walls more blank than ever?

To walk with fever. Nothing but
late night blue where voices

search for cover in woods gone
wild in the mind. No picnic

but those shirts stripped off
our backs. A makeshift feast.

Hellos. Good-byes. Useless acts
that fill up most of our lives.

Sestina

Bulging pockets seduced by a dance of dice
where winking widows let mascara bleed
down stiff lapels beside a crutch that bites
the hand that rocks a cradle's claire de lune,
chandeliers turned low as draughts of ghosts
rummage through a home that's up for sale—

a radio on the sill unable to revive "Come Sail
Away" for all those baby boomers who dice
up prom-night stories welling up with ghosts
of infidelities, even assholes bleeding
for some old fifties tune like "Blue Moon"
banged on a toy piano whose rusty notes bite

chromatic chords, all of us hungry for a bite
of whatever we can get—sailor boys for sale
down by the pier pinned beneath a full moon
where they squat as if to shit dead men's dice
rattling on rotten boards as musicians bleed
their instruments (how else summon ghosts

of the past?—Hart Crane dancing with the ghost
of Lowell last seen sailing a moonlit bight
where Bishop noticed "stains like dried blood
where ironwork had rusted"—Ouro Prêto for sale
the year she flew back North, wings de-iced
as she ducked behind winter's suicide moon

with earphones in her ears, the cries of loons
the closest she could get to Lota's ghost
still hovering over their abandoned paradise)
oh poesis poesis and all those megabytes
of memory lost inside some hard drive sold
down by the pier while our cursors bleed

into hypertext—chat-room boytoys with blood
on their hands renewed by dawn, the pale moon
but a hint of those crimson tides we sail
each night while that virus comes and goes
towards ghostly hands now waving goodbye—
too soon to tell whether old loves live or die.

Kiss and Tell

A bedroom slick with pearl where binoculars had been.

Or migrate to the porch for a game of kiss and tell.

Twice as many strokes it takes to get the well-hung off.

No dramamine to drown what weathervane unspun.

Nor touch the boy next door where cue balls crack.

Where the box fan's giant blades gently turn unplugged.

The basement of a church a phone unhooked look out.

A Mighty Fortress

The red shift finger of God closing in
on raccoons curled fetal under a cloud
of flies. Hoods drawn over stubbled chins
as churches are torched. Bites of sound
sandwiched between commercial breaks
overheard by our neighbors trading-in
their HBO for a satellite dish filliped
by anxiety. No pizzles hung out to dry,
only voices back-masked on white vinyl
as a diamond stylus skates away on its
cantilever—a polyester disco disaster
stuck in the groove again. Dear Reader—
there should be a picnic. A mind accused
of tawdry intent zooming-in on titty-
twisting fudge packers who circle-jerk
to the Tabernacle Choir as you suddenly
pull out—skid marks left under salacious
skies overtaken by the Great Salt Lake.

To Zion

Even passages from a Bible could not dictate
our behavior—Mormon Elders who would bless
the sacrament on Sunday dressed in black
polyester suits, eyeing eager boys to lure
them into closets—"Seven Minutes in Heaven"
a game we knew too well, we who were the salt

of the earth, leaving mouths with a salty
aftertaste. Our bishop a local dictator
in shiny boots, whip-crack promising heaven
for submissive penitents who were blessed
with public hugs and kisses he'd use to lure
us into his house, then bruising us black

and blue he'd recite from the worn black
covers of a pocket Book of Mormon, his salt-
and-pepper beard a halo around those lurid
lips he'd lick before he began to dictate
new commands: "Oh come on me and I will bless
thee with eternal life, an endless heaven

in the folds of my cloak." It was heaven
just to get out of there, threats of black-
mail hurled at us along with his blessing
up sore asses leaking tiny trails of salt
still burning in our cracks, throbbing dick
tattooed onto our flesh with such allure

we'd come back for more, trying to lure
a hoard of new initiates into his heavenly
clutches. For what is God if not a dictator
who kindly calls us home, and we the black
sheep of his fold eager to taste the salt
lick of his cock even as we learn to bless

the poor at heart who now recite "Blessed
Art Thous," already hooked on the barbed lure
of his sex—his sweat but stinging salt
in wounds that will not heal, hell our heaven
as we plunge headlong into that blackened
hole we call his glory, his enormous dic-

tatorial office where blessed angels take dic-
tation by the Great Salt Lake—our blackest
sins forgiven as he lures us all into heaven.

Kingdom Come

charcoal lines left on that canvas

where the border remains untouched

if only something harder yes there

without anxiety as the night began

where the border remains untouched

an open lap in the shape of a swan

without anxiety as the night began

unfolding itself under candlelight

an open lap in the shape of a swan

in a house that has grown enormous

unfolding itself under candlelight

brushes bleeding in a jar of water

in a house that has grown enormous

a canvas done with charcoal lines

brushes bleeding in a jar of water

that turned into the color of wine

An Inferno

Left unspoken in that din where the fuse got blown.

Wax fruit piled high an antique cut-glass bowl.

Or else forget that party not invited in.

Stroke mag strobes you smoke you megawatt throbbing pulse.

Headphones in on paths no one hear dare own.

Repeat selection random sampler hits.

As precinct protocols mirandize hotline overrides.

Nor photo-reduce a face to file claims.

To touch alone amazed still able to respond.

Lava lamp plugged in a room starting to lose its chill.

IV.

Ex Nihilo

A renewed taste for Voltaire / itinerant
artists selling their wares from door to door
under a seizure of atmospheric effects /
sunlight slashing through a curtain of cloud
to strike locations anyone could find
if they really wanted to start stalking us
through deepest sleep in a garden built
by hands / a rosebush washed in dew a site
for starter homes made out of trading
cards where voices congregate in some
enclosed unconscious world immune
to bright consumer packaging beyond
this world of so-called things / heavier
than vines those hours trying hard to bud
again / last year's artist another AIDS
inspired death as homage to sterility
each time the phone goes off / not fight nor
flight but mind as catacomb the catatonic
self retreats to a Virgin birth / a poem
pinned down / Giotto frescoes now reduced
to copies low on toner stuffed in student
sacks in order to situate ourselves in time
or space as long as surfaces dominate
the scene we're in dismantled by unseen
ants marching single file towards that edge.

In Fear

No roses in the house.
They were not needed—ashes

smeared across the door.
It was then I knew

he was serious. Cut stems
piled in a stainless sink—

roses I did not deserve.

*

And the room now filling
with otherness   open

open   the therapist says
a word so unlike brick

that flies through glass
with a magic-markered

message not to be ignored—

*

And if the poem should stop
writing itself, could I

still go on, the subject
having been exhausted?

Those wind chimes tinkling
when there is no wind—

sleep so easily disturbed.

Against Nature

Eight dollars for a dozen roses sold
on Christopher and Grove where another

fag was hunted down last night by some
fraternity boys who took their turns

with a pocket knife—a Village safari
kicking the bias death toll up a notch

or two. Boytoy hothouse flowers forced
to bloom too soon—their eyelids ringed

with bruise. More and more undercover
cops unloading into streets where neon

lipstick-strutting sluts blow kisses far
and wide. As weed to crack, so blood

to thrusting hips in vacant lots where
pissed-on corpses mark a warring turf.

Habeas Corpus

Wreathed in fair is fair, my mother's corpse traded-in
for an iced Manhattan more steady than a dumptruck's

beep while backing up uphill—a single body playing host
to haywire cells in that swelter of mink coats run amok

on every fire escape charbroiling steaks hung out to dry
for the Bronx's die-hard fans—ecstatic nothings scribbled

on the horizon line, the interstate but an asphalt ribbon
lacing up the tresses of a Jersey princess—baby's breath

sweeter than car exhaust choking her greasy diner locks
while sugar packets waterfall into a coffee mug the color

of sewer sludge oh Paterson with nails done up defying
trailer trash and anthrax-coated cactus needles lodged

inside a Zippo lighter aimed at the President or the Pope
while a mile-long-hysterical-stolen-handbag-squeal snakes

around City Hall for ransacked blocks where ghetto girls
wrapped up in moth-chewed scarves imported from Peru

kneel down hoi polloi on amber shards to pay obeisance
to patrol cars beckoning downtown precinct ride right on

past Hermana Iglesia decked out in Passaic Falls spilling
over that sea of votive candles the sacristan snuffs out.

Till Death Us Do Part

A tooth-torn hunk of pear rind sinking
to the bottom of my grappa. Silence
I chose but did not choose—your lips
the site of an old catastrophe. Brazen

as Federigo de Montefeltro demanding
for ransom a Hebrew Bible—unholy
vocalise erupting throughout the city's
festive bustle inside that dark cathedral

cooler than a cellar floor. A confession
in lieu of conversation. How you put on
such mighty airs that blot out sunlight
threaded-through the tapestry's tangled

underside. More than ready, you said,
for adoration, verbal frottage suffused
with hostile glamour rubbing off on me
like gold leaf. Touch me not, I cried

with eyes wide-open, glued to a swivel
monitor angling in on wedding cake
more than decades old thawed for this
occasion mirrored hundredfold beneath

the glare of a chandelier, the dog-eared
corners of connubial vows now pooling
at those margins *not meant to be read*—
such private remonstrations trumping up

fidelity to cruel remarks, signs of age
stumbling into sundry joints where cold
diurnal machinations forecast tirades
backboned by a hoarse anonymous toast.

Winter

Stalks of hacked-down corn poking through snow.

Wanting to replace or be replaced he said.

Bullets in slow-motion mapping the hunter's arc.

Where the compass fell a sign of distress.

A school of swollen tongues darting at his balls.

Frozen waterfalls embroidered onto silk.

Lodged inside his throat by the edge of the road.

A Rendezvous

Roses in a vase that centuries have sought.
His name as chaff as chattering husk scattered
On the loam darkened by autumn rains.
Oldies you did not request through gridlock
Six-o-clocked and steady as a holiday
Spree cut short in the slot of a faulty ATM.
Credit-card sluts in cyberspace awaiting
Silicate melt thinning into a molten glaze
Wherever bicarbonate mists fumigate
A kiln. A vase centuries have sought. A name.
A ski-masked face with ankles trouser-shackled
To the site. A double-winged Curtis "Jenny"
Inverted on perforated sheets (as shown)
Auctioned-off to the highest-flying bidder.
To the lowest chalk-white piece of ass
To hopscotch up that slippery slope plumped
With pillows where a tube of lube awaits—

Next Day

Between the cycles of wash and rinse, a song
about to be sung, all ears lulled by a radio
while toddlers teeth on disposable pens,
while lovers spill speed across the stones
of a glassed-in vivarium, lepidoptera at rest,
in flight, in dreams, each caught in a storm
of juvenile chatroom cyber smut soaking up
chronic carpal tunnel pixel by pixel, hypnotic
pre-dawn infomercial drone in exchange for
flat TV and digitized sound, our solitudes
wired into subterranean optic lines, decrypted
surge-protected codes cruising anonymous
glass abuzz with neon glow and embryonic
lexia languishing on a music stand, marginal
notes scribbled-out below the staff, below
the institutional clock face masking hours
in that brownout run ariot, your appetite
camouflaged in grunt fatigues dirtied-up
at the knees, a song about to be sung, daisy-
chained anxieties now horse-drawn through
a gas-lit park where the dread of connubial
bliss and miniscule tectonic shifts delivered
a tremor through the family skating rink—

Noli Me Tangere

Left out overnight a package on your porch.

As armored cars start slipping gears.

Ashes on an updraft floating up the flue.

That plastic jack-o-lantern full of sweets.

Or masquerade until the condom tears.

To bridge a seedy past a future yet unknown.

Leveled into rubble by just a single blast.

Some winter coats turned inside out.

A city we call love spread before our feet.

In Flagrante Delicto

I. Lethe

sound asleep and shadowed by a crumbling pier the body of a stranger

caught in such autoerotic repose and if that rowboat drowned in sand

fails to budge or moonlit sails proclaim the absence of an actual wind

what marriage do we have that thrives on was instead of is to be a kite

washed up on shore blackened shells strewn in trampled grass where

fires last night had been your kiss refused the taste of him ripped deep

inside the salt tide's aftermath inferno streaked eroding all remaining

sense of shore the dawn mere possibility where oarlock gently creaked

II. Like Boys Next Door

channel surfing from baseball scores to late night news for images

of ourselves in vain no faggots here in uniform only shirts that say

repent or perish as closets open wide their flaming doors just try on

the face of a christ that took a lifetime of our suffering to achieve

last-pick sissies striking out foreheads marked with ash as tongues

begin to slide like eels in public parks tempting boys who'd flock

to sport some jockstraps stuffed down throats where teeth had been

knocked-out a pack of trading-cards some drag from base to base

III. Just Some Boys

tossing frisbees in the eucalyptus scented air equidistant to the site

of old catastrophes waterlogged under a bridge our bodies pulled

to the center where it sags with years of connubial bliss and hardly

an hour's peace on unpaved roads that lead to a drive-thru window

where shrooms were tucked in a happy meal why not spy on boys

who spread their legs under leaves so green you'd think it was a set

heaving in the heat forget that homeless voice that kept on shouting

how many easter eggs you want up your ass the two of us pushing

IV. Roman Fever

gripped by a cell-phone panic day-trading shares a load more fun

than getting drunk on Jersey sky awash in amaretto light as I vespa

through the Palisades dependent more on Wall St. than the voice

of Pasolini now walling out all canyon echo clandestine rest-stop

action darting through the shrubs in search of Armani-suited cock

pack-muled through trails winking past patrol-car glare at dusk

that dogstar all aglitter over Ostia falling into the hands of rough

trade *che gelida mania* thread-bare boxers pulled down to our heels

V. Home of the Brave

reduced to rubble our democratic vistas unable to outlast far-right

terrorists who plan to poison water supplies as we wine and dine

in whistle stops trying to outbully operatic regicides curled inside

the tail of a treble clef floating on the outskirts of a forgotten town

where patriots bored from shooting at paper targets put complete

bomb-making guides online while orphans playing stick ball sift

through cases of crackerjack hit lists faxes anthrax sold by mail

some triggers and detonating fuses left inside that local ballot box

VI. Heavy Freight

a handprint fossilized on a child's startled face a bout of fisticuffs

as witness to love's excess straddling another bride as the bouquet

flies ferruginous tresses spilling over marble fonts into some abyss

eleemosynary grunts instead of sermons on the mount as grounds

for divorce where orphaned souls stampede down ungulated clefts

bikini wax ripped off depilatory forms to appease an ultramontane

satrap instructed in orthography by missionaries caught red-handed

in compromised positions trying to micturate into the rutilant night

VII. Requiem

a prayer pooling on our lips while semen spurts across the room

into the laps of virgins hitched in stirrups all of 'em ready to ride

some heavenly horse out of life while candles drip into sockets

of candied skulls that crown a gravestone pulverized by lichen

in a field where couples lean against a crumbling wall the sound

of iron sandals drawing near Andrei Rublev on a board between

two ladders erecting icons in the dark even as Cocteau's woman

wanders onto a set with eyes painted on her eyelids that are closed

VIII. Sirens Singing

of a lover's eyes newly-minted in maternal din anxieties complete

with pink fiestaware jarring the hours a hundredfold where vocal

mutilations hover over a violin come unstrung no talk only grunts

washed up on shore all those hag-infested hours redolent with fog

her laughter's rickety bridge seldom crossed emotions clocking in

instead of punching out the taste of it percolating on that stovetop

licked by dawn by way of telegram a truce delivered yet somehow

always the wrong address the come-on instead of a goodnight kiss

Walking Alone at Ocean's Edge

And the bottle washes up. Nor cruelly spoken where a blindman walks tapping code. Metronomic dawn striking ashen claves where you are an occidental ghost steaming up the sewer grates. As paramedic nights

tongued their way through asphalt hot from long-gone suns—ambition armored in its coat of flies. Tomorrow we die. And so on. Impenitent remarks whip-cracking into fanfare shriek. The hullabaloo of you

like spilled Shiraz. What parrots sundry thoughts, disrobed as we are in borrowed garb? The AC fan-belt working loose. Childhood a field of flood-swept corn where funnel clouds tore a hayloft off its hinges.

And so to roadside woods our nakedness has fled. As operatic registers rope-in herds of bucking steer more sturdy than our unsteady voices crashing against those foghorned shores in the jetsam time maroons.

V.

Ars Poetica

Fish are swimming at ease—
    this is the happiness of fish.
        But the sage kings are dead
    and the guarding of names has become
lax. Strange terms have risen
    and the names and actualities
        have become confused . . .
    When the pond dries up, all the fish
huddle close together
    and try to keep each other moist
        with their own spit—

Courtly Inscriptions Inked on Jute

No way in or out—decades of discord
laid out in monasteries instead
of mystical tracts. The *Ars Magna* kept

beside his bed, the Pyrenees an epic
all by itself. No need for frescoes
rescued from old churches on the hillsides

of Provence. Or maidenhead—lute notes
plucked on ravaged strings leaving
lines of blood down some ruined façade.

Splinters from the Tree That Lightning Struck

Amid the carved halls of spring
like two swallows who return

to the southern states, the mind
will arrive robed in sericeous

plumes of smoke as crickets leave
the walls of the house for good.

*

Wounded in his own house, his knees
brought low in that restless night—

fever seeping out through every pore.
And solitude came to reclaim him—

a blade of tempered steel still warm
in its sheath, eyes glazed with salt.

*

The star has not yet risen. Remain
in residence where the illness

shall be hidden. Wealth and silk
shall come of themselves—no need

to start your life again. Just walk
into the dark and be as Mount T'ai.

After the Funeral

Two dead spiders on the tile floor at dusk—
By dawn, the whole house would be swept.

Consolation

You're ashes now, no longer a corpse
in a hospital gown—jaundiced skin wrapped tight
    around jutting bone, regions within
        colonized by zones of black. They said a month,
    maybe a week, but the damage seemed
far off in the absence of human speech—
    requests for oxygen denied, nostrils
        drying out, your skin starting to itch wherever
    the body's salt accumulated
as your liver gave out, coin-size lesions doubling
    the morphine drip. And you so helpless
        as I once was swaddled in an amnion
    wrap, the forceps gripping down, backslap
ushering in the first breath. Now those pliant gates
    rust shut against all that grows within—
        a mother who leaves no legacy to steer
    our futures by. And yet these bones buried
underneath our own skin like a borrowed suit
    woven from threads unstrung in the garden
        of your death—floral wreaths garlanding a hearse
    while a pair of robins stand sentinel
on the mortuary lawn where that mural
    made by monks overlooks your remains—
        your resting place a sixteen-hundred dollar
    marble niche sealing the urn-ash in,
bone and gristle of your favorite Siamese
    sealed in there as well—unheard laughter
        loosening your grip where the call-button hung
    useless as the nurse unable to increase
your dosage in those final hours, invisible
    silk garrote tightening around your throat—
        around the silence that your life had become.

Ghost Ranch

Found herself in a world that left her
alone enough immersing hours in work
        that somehow made loneliness sound
                a lot like loveliness a palpable dream
        made possible by the receipt
of an inheritance over years continued
        to produce in spite of cormorants
                flying low among casitas frying up
        sopaipilla adrip with honey
before the advent of electricity
        and running water there on the edge
                of a wilderness beyond anyone's reach.

Georgia O'Keefe: American Icon

Announced to her playmate, "I'm going to be an artist."

Enrolled at Sacred Heart to receive instruction first.

Viewed an exhibition of controversial works on paper.

Discarded old materials and mannerisms to start anew.

Vacationed summers in the Sangre de Cristo Mountains.

Traded-in Penitente crosses for animal pelvic bones.

Abstracted nature but still relied on financial support.

Moved into an apartment overlooking Lexington Avenue.

Rejected Freudian notions focussed on her gender.

Invited by Dole Pineapple to produce a corporate ad.

Acquired three acres in Abiquiu an adobe house of course.

Suffered a partial loss—left only with peripheral sight.

Awarded a Presidential medal, the highest civilian honor.

Scattered on the desert floor at the age of ninety-eight.

Commemorated a decade later on a u.s. postage stamp.

Looking West

What are those magpies doing over there
picking up crusts I've scattered in the field
only to stack them neatly by that well
filled up with cement? All of it
done without a thought as a black ant
paddles in the toilet bowl, mesmerizing
the cat. So many books I'll never read—
a dusty weight making the bookshelves sag.

The Long Boat

A full-lipped flesh canoe floating downstream
to where the widows have gone. It took
some discipline to get that current going—
shrunken breasts flooding the world with light,
bellows quickening love's annunciation
of ash. The hours heavier than pomegranate
yet unable to alight. Only sores
festering there in the corners of the mouth
could anchor us to silence, the walls
cipher-scratched with calligraphic signs
we could not read as the crows in the yard
began to descend for a few last crusts tossed out
at dusk. None of us would be going back.

Emptying the Mind

Assuming the lotus, his ears and nostrils
sealed with wax, the rima glottidis
blocked by his tongue, Haridasa was slowly raised
like an ancient Buddha hewn from stone
then set inside a wooden box they buried
for forty days. His breath ceased. His pulse
undetectable at the wrists when they
finally dug him out, his bronzed skin
clean-shaven as pupils brought him back to life—

Sitting Naked on a Porch Facing
the Sangre de Cristo Mountains

My own semen quickening on the tongue
while a truckload full of wooden planks
pulls up the drive—one solitude impinging
on another till he spots me there at last

and slowly backs away. Hillside crosses
outlasting bones of conquistadors mark
a journey's end—flagellant processions
crying out to the *Sanguador* for lashes

equal to the five wounds of Christ, His
seven last words, even His forty days
in the wilderness for those who could stay
conscious long enough during the secret

rituals of Holy Week, actual nails used
at the chosen site—the workings of spirit
caught in the sound of sundry tools
strapped to a carpenter's belt on earth

as in heaven, each of us erecting crosses
alongside those desert roads set aside
for all the laddered reaches of the soul—
milk-white glaze as witness to dying forms.

Knowing When to Stop

Bathed in water, air, and fire, his summer
bride retires at night to a room buried
in the earth. No stones caught in sandals

from dusk to dawn, only Tseng Tzu's voice
haunting him: *what ten eyes behold, what
ten hands point to, isn't that frightening?*

Passing Through the Enchanted Circle

Blanketed under sage-gray skies, the afternoon steeped
in mountains brindled with piñon
    and pine as the horizon thins to mottled foothills
        where the road bends—the aspen-
thickened canyon igniting spring's late fires, a hawk
shifting his weight from one wing
    to the other beside a cliff shorn away by gusts
        that swept across those lava-
            blackened mesas thunderstruck while we slept—
        arms in corpse position, a wasp
ensnared in the static nest of a widow's hair splayed
across her pillow, her hands
    immobilized in a dreamscape full of clouds shifting
        shape, all of America starved
    for the desert's brutal modesty stripping our wants
to the simplest forms—skull
    and arrowhead governed by the same unspoken laws.

A Minor Distraction

To chart the body's pull away from text—
from *Wuthering Heights* to the *Analects*,
hoping you might call. He says he can't
get the boy to stop calling—must be love
or something. Fingering my ass, I read
alone, often wanting to be someone else.

Easter, 1997

Hand in hand down a sun-washed street, two men
tempting fate with smiles that open wide
to a wild peal of bells. Fear hidden
out of view where the disintegration begins.
A flock of ski-masked boys smoking
on the doorsteps of a church, crushed matches
underfoot. Christ roiling in the blood
while two-by-fours descend like crows to carrion—

Approaching the Buddha

Binoculars left in the backseat
of your car. Tread marks leading
to a flattened toad with flies
crawling over it. Those pagodas
in the distance somehow made
a difference—joss sticks stuck
in giant urns burnishing the air.

Many Mansions

Lacking gravitas, disillusioned yuppies congregate
in a faux-Etruscan theater, acting out our appetite
for concatenating tactics intended to shock
a brazenly chic high-styled public hardly fungible
for such epiphanic free falls lodged inside
a fissure where nothingness steadily blooms,
halcyon sophisticates parading second-hand hauteur
amid all that ambient razzmatazz abuzz inside
a media-mogul hell nudging us into recklessness—
hortatory slogans fit for anorexic teens passing
entire winter months in bed to keep caloric
expenditures down till spring's explosive riot
of floralia takes root, preening eyes afire
with a weakness for amassing iconographic
bric-a-brac and excess schlock—acrolithic masks
unearthed at sites by *tombaroli* declared
persona non grata plundering troves so Victorian
in their clutter—*objets d'art* beautiful but mute—
the Euphronios krater cooling-off in a Swiss vault.

Middle-Class Realia as Iconographic Vanitas

Desire zeroing-in on that Furby eBay auction
    while smut chat gets caught up
in the Hegelian carpet roll—the secrets of your life
    scrawled on Post-it notes that fell
off of your dash—a pack of Lucky Strikes stairmastered into
    Liberty's verdigrised torch—
Ellis Island heavier than an oil freighter grounded
    in Coos Bay, grenade bundles
dropped into the cargo hold where stowaways and rough trade
    are peddled inside a dream
disfigured by grief, our heels on poesy's throat, our wants
    enclosed in the Dantesque windows
of Saks Fifth Avenue where pigeons peck at dried-out crusts
    like fifty-something biddies
trying to take their power back, their bulging pocketbooks
    a Bakhtinian carnival
scatterpiece hauled away by troika or by gitney ride
    through Central Park—tenderness
staged beside Ming vases of doubtful provenance that puts
    everything on its mettle
from the prints of Lorrain to the odes of Keats—not buying
    the house but buying the view—
the zazen of stained glass undoing ambition's talons
    claw by claw—stocks and futures
traded-in for a Byzantine reliquary housing splinters
    and a nail from the True Cross.

Reading the Book of Odes Late at Night, I Turn out the Light and Go on Reading

Though the ceiling looks down on you, be
free from shame in the confines of your own
home. It's not about what is seen but what is
known in the mind. Though white fish die
and lie at bottom, they still are clearly seen.

Western Wars Mitigated by the Analects

Illegal fund raising and espionage attempting to ignite
new suspicions: "In a war with China, which side would you
take?" a neighbor asks, each of us rounded-up into camps
from the trenches of war-torn Europe to the smart bombs
of the Gulf fueling the massive engine of American success—
when the root is established, the law will grow, history
as it really happened—rifle toting hunters storming onto
bleachers at the gym where last night's game was won—
as a thing is cut and filed, as a thing is carved and polished,
machine-gun fire of the underline key on a student's
Smith-Corona but *a correspondence of words and action,
of name and actuality* while voices keep directing airstrikes
on Iraqi positions drowned by strong revanchist passions—
Rosie Riveter sent back home to assist in our nation's
baby-boom from anti-business animus to economic
renaissance where we were in for "a nice little shoot-'em up,"
hey, hey, LBJ, how many kids did you kill today?—
*to fish with a line but not a net, nor shoot a bird
at rest*, Matthew Shepard the latest hate-crime poster child—
to go too far is the same as not going far enough,
the carcass of James Byrd but an act of "animal
cruelty" posted on that web site "for Whites only"—a Klan
cartoon of newlyweds driving off from church to bedlam
with two blacks tied to their bumper—*in the morning go
and gather grass, in the evening twist your ropes* as China's
Most-Favored-Nation Status undergoes House review, stalled
peace talks ushering restless ground troops in—*the best
course is to establish virtue, the next best is to establish
achievement, and the next best after that to establish words.*

Library of Congress Cataloging-in-Publication Data

Liu, Timothy.
    Hard evidence / Timothy Liu.
        p. cm.
    ISBN 1-58498-023-0 (cloth : alk. paper) -- ISBN 1-58498-022-2 (pbk. : alk. paper)
    1. Gay men--Poetry. 2. Asian Americans--Poetry. I. Title.

PS3562.I799 H37 2001
811'.54--dc21

                                                        2001027313

Designed by
Samuel Retsov

Text: 12 pt Minion

acid-free paper

Printed by
McNaughton & Gunn